Product Management Blueprint: Navigating the Road to Mastery

A Comprehensive Tutorial for Aspiring and

Established Product Leader

By Web Maverick

Chapter 1: Discovering Product Management Strategies

Introduction

In today's rapidly evolving business landscape, mastering cutting-edge product management tools and techniques is paramount for achieving organizational excellence. Whether you are a seasoned expert or a newcomer in the field, this comprehensive manual will unveil practical methods and strategies to thrive in the dynamic realm of product management.

What Is Product Management?

Product management encompasses the end-to-end process of conceiving, developing, launching, and maintaining products. It's the art and science of transforming ideas into tangible solutions that meet customer needs while driving business growth.

Unveiling the Essence of Product Management

Product management stands as the linchpin of the entire product lifecycle, encompassing the intricate journey from ideation to maintenance. It blends innovation and methodology to translate abstract ideas into groundbreaking solutions that not only meet customer demands but also drive business growth. Let's delve deeper into the essential components:

1. Redefining Product Management:

    - Product management emerges as a pivotal strategic function that steers the complete product journey.

    - It requires a profound comprehension of market trends, customer expectations, and organizational goals.

    - Product managers serve as visionary innovators who bridge the gap between concept and reality, shaping the future of products.

1. Exploring Focus Areas:

- Internal Innovation:

    - Beyond customer-centric products, product management extends to creating internal tools and solutions.

- This involves streamlining processes, optimizing operational efficiency, and fostering a culture of creativity.

- Examples include state-of-the-art HR management systems, advanced CRM platforms, and streamlined ERP solutions.

- **External Excellence:**

  - This aspect revolves around crafting bespoke products and services tailored to meet external customer needs.

  - From luxury cosmetics to secure payment gateways, the spectrum of offerings is diverse and extensive.

1. Harnessing Innovative Structures and Frameworks:

- **Tailored Approaches for Different Company Sizes:**

  - Startups often embrace lean product management structures to enable agility and rapid innovation.

  - In contrast, large corporations may adopt complex hierarchies with multiple VP roles and specialized divisions.

- **Dynamic Reporting Mechanisms:**

- o Product managers may directly engage with the CEO or senior leadership to ensure strategic alignment.
- o Alternatively, they could integrate within cross-functional teams or distinct business units for enhanced collaboration.

1. Mastering Upstream and Downstream Operations:

- Upstream Strategic Focus:
  - o Involves strategic planning, roadmap conceptualization, and exploration of cutting-edge concepts.
  - o Aligning product vision with overarching corporate strategies for cohesive growth.

- Downstream Lifecycle Management:
  - o Encompasses overseeing the complete product lifecycle from growth to decline phases.
  - o Collaborating with marketing, sales, and post-launch support teams to drive sustained success.

Embark on an enlightening journey to explore the advanced dimensions of product management through actionable insights and practical examples. Let's embark on creating a sample project to apply these concepts in a simulated

real-world scenario.

Chapter 2: The Evolving Role of a Product Manager: Navigating the Product Landscape

Introduction

Welcome to the immersive journey through The Evolving Role of a Product Manager. This guide is designed to provide you with a deep understanding of the intricate world of product management, offering practical insights and empowering you to excel in this dynamic field, whether you are just beginning your career or are a seasoned professional.

Exploring the Dynamic Realm of Product Management

Product managers play a vital role in the success of products and services, acting as the driving force behind their development and performance in the market. Let's explore the key responsibilities that define their role:

Product Planning:

- Customer-Centric Approach:
  - Product managers dive deep into understanding customer desires, preferences, and pain points,

utilizing advanced tools like sentiment analysis and predictive analytics to anticipate needs.

- o By listening to the voice of the customer, they decode what truly resonates with the target audience.

- Market Intelligence Mastery:

  - o Keeping a pulse on emerging market trends, competitor strategies, and disruptive technologies to craft innovative product solutions that align with the ever-changing landscape.

  - o Utilizing cutting-edge tools such as AI-driven market analysis platforms to gain a competitive edge.

Holistic Focus on Internal and External Strategies:

- Internal Innovation:

  - o Developing customized tools and solutions for internal use, such as advanced HRIS systems and AI-powered CRM platforms, to streamline operations and boost organizational efficiency.

- External Product Development:

  - o Creating a diverse range of products and services for external customers, spanning physical goods like smart devices to digital offerings such as blockchain solutions and AR/VR applications.

Data-Driven Decision Intelligence:

- Harnessing the power of big data analytics to drive strategic product decisions, leveraging predictive modelling and machine learning algorithms to optimize product performance.

- Balancing the diverse needs of cross-functional teams through data-driven insights and collaborative decision-making processes.

Product Leadership and Ownership:

- Visionary Stewards:

  o Acting as the visionary architects of products, product managers take on the responsibility of ensuring the long-term success and relevance of the offerings.

  o Constantly monitoring the competitive landscape, identifying market gaps, and capitalizing on emerging opportunities to stay ahead of the curve.

Crafting a Strategic Product Roadmap:

- Visionary Roadmapping:

- Developing a comprehensive roadmap that outlines the product's journey from ideation to launch, incorporating elements like target launch dates, user segments, and feature prioritization.

- Influencing Stakeholders:

  - Collaborating with senior executives to align product strategies with organizational goals, advocating for the resources and support needed to drive successful product outcomes.

Exploring Customer-Centric Strategies in Product Management

Welcome to the immersive world of The Evolving Role of a Product Manager, where we unravel the art of shaping exceptional products and services through a customer-centric lens. Let's embark on this enlightening journey together, exploring strategies that drive product success.

Unveiling Competitive Insights and Customer Personas

Competitive Intelligence Insights:

- Proactive Competitive Analysis:

- Stay ahead of the competition by monitoring their moves, identifying strengths and weaknesses, and leveraging competitor insights to drive product enhancements and innovations.
- Embrace a culture of continuous improvement through competitive benchmarking and analysis tools.

Empathy-Driven Customer Understanding:

- Persona Profiling:
  - Dive deep into customer personas to understand their motivations, challenges, and aspirations, utilizing advanced data analytics tools to create rich user profiles.
  - By segmenting users based on behaviour and preferences, product managers can tailor solutions that resonate with diverse customer segments.

Insightful Data Visualization:

- Data-Driven Persona Creation:
  - Gather actionable insights through surveys, interviews, and focus groups to create data-driven customer personas that reflect real user needs and preferences.

- o Meet Sarah:

- o Persona Name: Sarah

- o Background: 30-year-old marketing professional based in New York.

- o Goal: To enhance brand visibility through innovative digital marketing strategies.

- o Challenge: Navigating the competitive digital landscape to drive customer engagement.

- o Potential Bias: Favors long-term brand building strategies over short-term gains.

Crafting a Strategic Roadmap: Navigating Your Product's Journey

Product Planning:

- Customer-Centric Roadmapping:
  - o Develop a roadmap that aligns with customer needs and market trends, leveraging advanced market research tools and user feedback mechanisms.
- Strategic Market Positioning:

- Anticipate market shifts and consumer preferences to steer product development in the right direction, ensuring alignment with future market demands.

Product Ownership Excellence:

- Visionary Product Leadership:

  - Act as the custodian of your product's success, championing its vision and purpose while adapting to evolving market dynamics and customer expectations.

  - Inspired by Tony:

  - Our hypothetical product manager, Tony, embodies strategic foresight and adaptability in navigating complex market landscapes.

Roadmap Execution Mastery:

- **Strategic Implementation:**

  - Translate your product roadmap into actionable initiatives, defining milestones, timelines, and success metrics to track progress and drive product success.

- **Stakeholder Alignment:**

  - Influence key stakeholders by articulating the value and impact of your product strategy, fostering cross-functional collaboration and support for successful execution.

Chapter 3: Product Manager Skills

In this comprehensive guide, we'll explore the essential skills that every product manager should possess. Whether you're an aspiring product manager or a seasoned professional, these insights will help you excel in your role.

1. Business Acumen: Navigating the Landscape

Business acumen is the cornerstone of effective product management. Here's what it entails:

Critical Thinking: Understand the market dynamics, customer needs, and organizational goals.

Research Savvy: Dive into market trends, technological advancements, and political landscapes.

Customer Connection: Bridge the gap between product and customer perspectives.

Negotiation: Sometimes, even the best ideas need negotiation with senior management.

2. Curiosity, Creativity, and Innovation

Curiosity: Stay curious about industry trends, emerging technologies, and user behaviour.

Creativity: Think outside the box to solve complex problems.

Innovation: Disrupt the status quo and explore novel approaches.

3. Communication: The Art of Connection

Verbal and Written Skills: Communicate effectively with stakeholders, engineers, and designers.

User-Centric Thinking: Step into users' shoes to shape products that resonate.

Data Processing: Analyse large datasets swiftly for informed decision-making.

4. Emotional Intelligence and Soft Skills

- Empathy: Understand users' emotions and needs.
- Self-Awareness: Recognize your strengths and areas for growth.
- Social Skills: Collaborate seamlessly with cross-functional teams.
- Time Management: Juggle multiple tasks efficiently.
- Leadership: Inspire and guide your team.
- Problem Solving: Tackle challenges head-on.

5. Technical Skills: Know Your Product Inside Out

- Product Knowledge: Understand your product's technical aspects.

- Collaboration Tools: Master tools like Microsoft Office, Teams, Zoom, WebEx, Slack, Mural, Trello, and Jira.

- Requirements Writing: Craft clear feature requirements for engineers.

- Time Management: Prioritize tasks effectively.

6. Domain Expertise: Understand Your Customer

- Domain Awareness: Dive deep into your product's domain (e.g., DevOps, healthcare, finance).

- User-Centric Design: Always think from the user's perspective.

- Presentations: Create compelling presentations for diverse audiences, from low-level to C-suite executives.

Remember, product management is a dynamic blend of technical prowess, soft skills, and strategic thinking. As you embark on this journey, keep learning, adapting, and honing your skills.

Chapter 4: Exploring Advanced Product Management Tools:

Let's dive into the exciting world of product management tools and strategies that are currently making waves in the industry. In this chapter, we will explore practical and cutting-edge tools that can elevate your skills and help you excel in real-world projects. Not only will we make learning engaging and easy, but we will also provide you with a unique sample project that is exclusive to this guide. Our goal is to ensure that you grasp these concepts without feeling overwhelmed, and we'll walk you through how to apply them in real projects.

Uncovering the Essence of Products: A Practical Guide

Products are not just items on a shelf; they are solutions that cater to specific needs or desires. From physical goods to services and beyond, understanding the essence of products is crucial in delivering value to consumers. Product management entails crafting effective strategies and informed decisions to ensure that a product meets its target audience's needs and thrives in a competitive market.

Exploring the Multifaceted Nature of Products:

- Beyond Tangibility: Let's explore everyday products like smartphones and laptops, as well as niche items such as smart home devices and wearable tech.

- Business-to-Business Dynamics: Delve into the intricacies of products designed for commercial use, requiring unique branding and marketing approaches.

The Product Journey: Extending Past the Sale

A customer's interaction with a product goes beyond just buying it:

- Pre-Purchase Engagement: Discover the various touchpoints that influence a customer's decision-making process, from social media recommendations to captivating ads.

- Post-Purchase Experience: Learn how products become integrated into customers' lives, leading to potential upgrades and repeat purchases.

Enhancing Offerings: The Role of Services

Explore the world of intangible services and their impact on user experiences:

- Service Excellence: Experience firsthand how services like online streaming platforms and subscription services enhance customer satisfaction.

Navigating the Product Manager's Role

Product managers are the architects behind successful product ecosystems:

- Product Classification: Dive into managing consumer goods, specialized products, and business-to-business offerings.

- Embracing Innovation: Stay ahead of the curve in the ever-evolving IT landscape and commit to continuous learning for future success.

Empowering Your Journey with Advanced Tools and Frameworks

Arm yourself with cutting-edge tools and methodologies for product development:

Design Thinking: Drive innovation and problem-solving by placing the user at the heart of product design. By empathizing with users, you can create products that truly resonate with their needs and desires. For example, imagine designing a mobile app for a food delivery service. By using design thinking, you would conduct interviews and observations to understand the pain points and preferences of both customers and delivery drivers. This approach could lead to features like real-time order tracking or personalized recommendations, enhancing the overall user experience.

Lean Startup Methodology: Validate your product ideas swiftly and effectively to reduce risks and maximize success. This methodology emphasizes building a minimum viable product (MVP) to gather feedback from real users early on. For instance, if you were developing a new social networking platform, you could create a basic version with essential features and release it to a small group of beta testers. Their feedback would help you iterate and improve the product iteratively, saving time and resources in the long run.

Customer Journey Mapping: Gain insights into how customers interact with your product throughout their entire experience. By visualizing each touchpoint, you can identify pain points and opportunities for enhancement. Take the example of an e-commerce website. By mapping out the customer journey from browsing products to making a purchase and receiving support, you can streamline processes, improve user satisfaction, and ultimately boost sales.

SWOT Analysis: Analyze your product's strengths, weaknesses, opportunities, and threats to make well-informed decisions and strategic plans. This tool helps you understand your competitive position in the market and anticipate potential challenges. For instance, if you were launching a new fitness app, conducting a SWOT analysis could reveal strengths like a unique workout algorithm, weaknesses such as limited marketing budget, opportunities like partnering with influencers for promotion, and threats like emerging competitors.

Conclusion

- Embrace the diverse range of products and services to enhance your product management skills and adaptability.

- Select tools and frameworks that align perfectly with your product's specific needs and goals.

- Maintain agility, innovation, and dedication to shaping the future of product management.

Embark on this exciting journey of exploration and innovation in product management, where creativity meets strategy to deliver memorable experiences for your target audience. Keep pushing boundaries, stay open to change, and develop products that stand out in the ever-evolving market landscape.

Product Life Cycle :

This guide will simplify the journey of a product from its inception to its retirement, highlighting the essential roles of product managers.

1) Introduction Phase:

The journey of a product in the market kicks off with the Introduction phase. At this point, it's crucial to understand what customers want, establish the product's vision, and oversee its development and launch. Product managers are key players here, creating sales and marketing strategies and targeting early adopters to boost the product's success.

To dive deeper into practical and cutting-edge tools trending in product management, let's explore advanced technologies like artificial intelligence (AI) and machine learning. These tools offer valuable insights into consumer behaviour, market trends, and product performance. For instance, AI-powered analytics platforms can assist product managers in making data-informed decisions by analysing extensive customer data.

In real-world projects, leveraging tools such as JIRA for project management and Trello for task organization can significantly boost productivity and efficiency. These project management tools facilitate effective team collaboration, progress tracking, and meeting deadlines in an organized manner.

Let's craft a unique sample project to showcase the application of these tools in a practical setting. Imagine developing a novel mobile application for a fitness tracking service. We can utilize JIRA to set up a project board with tasks like designing the user interface, integrating tracking algorithms, and performing beta testing. Concurrently, Trello can be employed to assign tasks to team members, establish deadlines, and monitor the progress at each development stage.

By integrating these advanced tools and methodologies into real projects, product managers can streamline workflows, enhance decision-making processes, and drive successful product launches.

2) Growth Phase:

In the Growth phase of a product's lifecycle, the emphasis shifts towards expanding market reach and meeting rising demand. Product managers intensify marketing initiatives and adjust strategies to sustain the product's growth momentum. This stage is crucial for securing a larger market share and ensuring continued success.

To navigate this phase effectively and stay ahead in the competitive landscape, leveraging practical and advanced trending tools is essential. Incorporating cutting-edge tools can streamline processes, boost efficiency, and empower product managers to make informed decisions swiftly. Let's explore some trending tools that can be instrumental in driving growth and success in real projects:

1. **AI-powered Analytics Platforms**: Utilizing advanced analytics tools powered by artificial intelligence can provide valuable insights into consumer behaviour, market trends, and performance metrics. For example, tools like Google Analytics and Mixpanel offer sophisticated analytics capabilities to track user engagement and conversion rates.

2. **Marketing Automation Software**: Implementing marketing automation tools such as HubSpot or Marketo can help streamline marketing campaigns, personalize customer interactions, and nurture leads efficiently. These tools automate repetitive tasks, optimize workflows, and enhance overall marketing effectiveness.

3. **Collaboration Platforms**: Leveraging collaboration tools like Slack or Microsoft Teams facilitates seamless communication and project coordination among team members. These platforms enable real-time collaboration, file sharing, and task management, enhancing productivity and ensuring project success.

4. **Project Management Tools**: Utilizing project management tools like Asana or Trello can aid in organizing tasks, setting deadlines, and tracking project progress effectively. These tools offer visual project management features, task prioritization, and team collaboration functionalities to ensure smooth project execution.

By integrating these innovative tools into your workflow, you can streamline operations, optimize performance, and drive growth in real projects. Let's create a sample project scenario to demonstrate how these tools can be applied in a practical setting:

Sample Project: Enhancing Customer Engagement Campaign

- **Objective**: Increase customer engagement and loyalty through targeted marketing initiatives.

- **Tools Used**:
  - AI-powered Analytics Platform (e.g., Google Analytics)
  - Marketing Automation Software (e.g., HubSpot)
  - Collaboration Platform (e.g., Slack)
  - Project Management Tool (e.g., Trello)

- **Execution**:
  a. Utilize AI analytics to identify key customer segments and preferences.
  b. Implement personalized marketing campaigns using automation tools.
  c. Coordinate campaign activities and share updates through collaboration platforms.

d. Track project milestones and monitor performance using project management tools.

e. Analyse results, iterate strategies, and optimize campaigns for continuous improvement.

By following this structured approach and leveraging advanced tools effectively, you can enhance customer engagement, drive growth, and excel as a professional product manager. Stay updated with the latest trends and tools to remain competitive and achieve success in your projects.

3) Maturity Phase:

During the Maturity phase of a product, it is crucial for product managers to leverage practical and advanced trending tools to sustain the product's growth and competitiveness in the market. Let's explore some interesting tools that can be beneficial for managing products in this phase in an easy-to-understand manner.

One popular tool that product managers can use is A/B testing software like Optimizely or VWO. This tool allows them to test different versions of their product features or marketing strategies to see which ones users like best. By looking at the results of these tests, product managers can make smart decisions based on data to make their product more appealing and user-friendly.

Another helpful tool is customer feedback analytics platforms such as Medallia or Qualtrics. These tools help product managers collect and analyse customer feedback on a large scale. This feedback helps them understand what users like, what issues they have, and how to make the product better. By listening to customers and incorporating their feedback into product decisions, managers can keep the product up-to-date and meet users' changing needs.

Let's imagine a project in the Maturity phase, like a mobile productivity app, to see how these tools can be used. Suppose the product manager wants to improve user engagement and retention rates. With A/B testing software, the manager can run tests on different ways to introduce new users to the app or on different features to see which ones keep users coming back.

By using customer feedback analytics platforms, the product manager can gather feedback from users on their experiences with the app. For instance, if users mention that they find it hard to navigate the app, the manager can focus on redesigning the app's layout to make it easier to use.

By including these tools in their work, professionals can make better decisions, create great user experiences, and make their products successful in the Maturity phase. This not only improves a product manager's skills but also gives them the tools they need to stand out in a competitive market.

4) Decline Phase:

In the Decline phase, products face reduced demand due to new trends or technological shifts. Product managers must then manage the product's gradual exit from the market, while also preparing for future innovations.

Throughout all these stages, product managers are the vigilant overseers, ensuring the product's performance aligns with goals and market demands. They collaborate with various teams, using insights from data to make informed strategic decisions and secure the product's place in the market.

To sum up, the product's life cycle is a four-phase process that requires skilled management and foresight. As we explore this topic further, you'll gain a deeper understanding of each phase and how to effectively navigate them.

The Seven Phases of the Product Management Lifecycle

The product management lifecycle is the journey a product takes, from a spark of an idea to its eventual retirement. Understanding these stages is crucial for any aspiring product manager, and this guide will take you through each phase, highlighting practical tools and real-world examples to make learning engaging and relevant.

1) Conceive Phase: Brainstorming and Building a Case

This phase is all about identifying opportunities and building a strong case for your product. Here's how to make it interesting:

Run Brainstorming Sessions:

Use collaborative online whiteboards like Miro to gather ideas from diverse teams.

Tools: Miro (https://miro.com/), Crazy Egg (https://www.crazyegg.com/)

Real-World Example: Imagine a company that makes fitness trackers. They identify a gap in the market for a tracker specifically designed for children.

Conduct User Research with a Twist:

Go beyond surveys. Utilize heatmap tools like Crazy Egg to understand how users interact with competitor products, identifying potential pain points your solution can address.

During the initial Conceive phase, the product manager evaluates whether a new product is feasible. They conduct thorough market research and a SWOT analysis to assess the company's strengths and the challenges it may face. This phase involves documenting various strategies to address market needs.

Once strategies are outlined, the product manager selects the best approach and seeks approval to move forward with a product concept. They may also create a prototype using 3D printing to visualize the product. Additionally, a marketing plan is crafted, though it's common to encounter some resistance at this stage.

2) Plan Phase:

Exploring Advanced Trending Tools and Techniques for Real Projects

In the Plan phase of a project, it's essential to utilize practical advanced tools that can elevate your work to the next level. Let's delve into some trending tools that can make your project both interesting and effective, while preparing you to tackle real-world challenges like a pro.

Product Roadmap Creation with Aha!: Aha! is a powerful tool that allows you to visually map out your product roadmap, detailing features, timelines, and dependencies. This tool helps in aligning your team towards a common goal and provides a clear direction for product development.

Business Model Analysis with Business Model Canvas: To ensure the viability of your project, tools like the Business Model Canvas can help you analyse different aspects of your business model such as value proposition, revenue streams, and cost structure. This tool assists in refining your business strategy for optimum success.

Marketing Strategy Design using HubSpot: HubSpot offers a suite of tools for inbound marketing, including content creation, social media management, and analytics. By leveraging HubSpot, you can create targeted marketing campaigns that resonate with your audience and drive results.

Prototyping with Figma: Figma is a popular design tool that facilitates collaborative prototyping and wireframing. It enables teams to create interactive prototypes, gather feedback, and iterate quickly, ensuring the final product meets user expectations.

Project Management with Asana: Asana is a versatile project management tool that aids in task assignment, progress tracking, and team collaboration. By utilizing Asana, you can streamline project workflows, enhance communication, and meet project deadlines efficiently.

Sample Project:

Imagine developing a mobile app for a fitness tracker that gamifies exercise routines. By utilizing Aha! for roadmap planning, Business Model Canvas for revenue analysis, HubSpot for marketing strategies, Figma for prototyping, and Asana for project management, you can create a comprehensive plan for executing this project successfully.

By incorporating these advanced tools into your projects, you can enhance productivity, foster innovation, and pave the way for professional growth. Embrace these tools, explore their functionalities, and witness how they transform your project management approach for the better.

3) Develop Phase:

In the Develop phase, the focus shifts to constructing the product and refining its design. The team updates strategies and finalizes an implementation plan. Quality assurance processes are initiated to ensure the product meets customer standards. Regular testing is conducted to confirm both the product's specifications and its usability. The launch plan is finalized, including pricing and promotional strategies, and customer support materials are prepared.

4) Qualify Phase:

The Qualify phase is a critical testing stage where the product is introduced to the market for initial feedback. This pre-launch period is essential for fine-tuning the product based on user input. The company must decide whether to proceed with the launch or address any significant issues that could warrant postponing or even discontinuing the project.

5) Launch Phase:

During the Launch phase, the team finalizes the launch strategy, ensuring all preparations are thorough. They assess potential risks and develop plans to mitigate them. Marketing materials are also finalized, setting the stage for the product's introduction to the market.

6) Deliver Phase:

In the Deliver phase, the focus shifts to the product's performance and reception in the market. The team monitors the product closely, making necessary adjustments and responding to new insights. This phase is dynamic, with continuous updates and changes to the product based on real-world use.

7) Retire Phase:

Planning for the Retire Phase in Product Management

In product management, the Retire phase marks the planning for the product's end-of-life. It involves crucial decisions on discontinuing support, terminating contracts, and managing the transition as the product becomes outdated.

Key Points to Consider in the Retire Phase:

- **Timeline Establishment:** Determine a clear timeline for phasing out support and services for the product.

- **Contract Termination:** Plan the termination of contracts related to the product, ensuring a smooth transition for all stakeholders.

- **Transition Management:** Develop strategies to manage the transition as the product reaches its end-of-life stage.

Advanced Trending Tools for Product Management:

1. **Tableau:** Tableau is a powerful data visualization tool that helps in analysing product performance metrics and making informed decisions.

2. **JIRA:** JIRA is a popular project management tool that aids in tracking tasks and issues related to product development and retirement.

Sample Project Scenario:

Imagine a scenario where a software company is planning to retire one of its legacy products. The product team collaborates with the sales and support teams to establish a timeline for discontinuation, notify existing clients, and migrate users to newer solutions seamlessly.

By utilizing tools like Tableau for analysing customer usage data and JIRA for tracking transition tasks, the team successfully navigates the Retire phase while ensuring minimal disruption to clients.

Working on Real Projects:

In real projects, product managers play a pivotal role in guiding the Retire phase. They must communicate effectively with cross-functional teams, monitor progress closely, and adapt strategies based on evolving circumstances to ensure a successful product retirement.

By incorporating advanced tools and following best practices, product managers can streamline the retirement process, mitigate risks, and drive sustainable outcomes for both the business and its customers.

Product Manager's functional areas:

In an organization, the term 'functional areas' refers to different departments or teams that handle specific responsibilities and tasks. These teams are essential for overseeing various aspects of the business, each with its unique functions. Product managers are crucial individuals who collaborate with these teams to ensure the successful development, launch, and management of a product.

They work closely with these teams, gathering valuable insights, coordinating efforts, and ensuring that the product aligns with the company's overall goals and strategies.

Apart from the traditional functional areas like engineering, marketing, sales, manufacturing, operations, customer support, project management, and distribution channels, modern product managers also need to be well-versed in utilizing advanced and trending tools to enhance their capabilities and efficiency in real-world projects.

One such trending tool is agile project management software like Jira or Trello, which enables product managers to streamline project workflows, track progress, and collaborate effectively with cross-functional teams. By mastering these tools, product managers can ensure that projects are delivered on time and within budget.

In addition, incorporating data analytics tools such as Google Analytics or Mixpanel can provide valuable insights into user behaviour, preferences, and product performance. By leveraging data-driven decision-making, product managers can optimize product features and marketing strategies for better customer engagement and retention.

Furthermore, familiarity with prototyping tools like Sketch or Adobe XD can facilitate the visual representation of product ideas, allowing product managers to quickly iterate and gather feedback from stakeholders before moving into full-scale development.

To illustrate, let's consider a sample project scenario where a product manager is tasked with launching a new mobile app. By utilizing agile project management software, the product manager can create a detailed project roadmap, assign tasks to different teams, and track progress in real-time. Data analytics tools can help in analysing user interactions within the app, identifying popular features, and optimizing user experience. Prototyping tools can aid in creating interactive mock-ups of the app interface, enabling stakeholders to visualize the final product before coding begins.

By incorporating these advanced tools and techniques into their skill set, product managers can navigate complex projects more efficiently, make informed decisions, and drive successful product outcomes in today's competitive market landscape.

To work effectively as a product manager and excel in guiding projects to success, one must master a variety of advanced tools and methodologies that are currently trending in the industry. These tools not only enhance productivity but also streamline processes for efficient project management and product development.

Let's delve into some practical and cutting-edge tools that can elevate your skills as a product manager:

Computer-Aided Design (CAD) software: This tool is essential for engineers to draft detailed designs with precision. By mastering CAD software, product managers can collaborate effectively with engineering teams and ensure the accurate visualization of product concepts.

User Experience (UX) Design tools: Improving user interactions with websites and applications is crucial for product success. Understanding and utilizing UX design tools will enable product managers to create user-friendly interfaces that resonate with the target audience.

Lean methodology: Focused on eliminating waste and optimizing processes, Lean methodology is a valuable approach for enhancing efficiency in product development.

Product managers can apply Lean principles to streamline workflows and deliver high-quality products promptly.

Design for Six Sigma (DFSS): This framework is dedicated to developing new products with minimal defects. By incorporating DFSS practices, product managers can ensure the quality and reliability of products from inception to launch.

Agile methodology: Agile offers a flexible approach to project management, allowing teams to adapt to changing requirements swiftly. Product managers proficient in Agile can lead cross-functional teams effectively and drive iterative development cycles for rapid product delivery.

To work effectively with these tools in real projects, let's consider a sample scenario:

Imagine you are leading a team to develop a new mobile application for a tech startup. As a product manager, you utilize CAD software to create detailed wireframes and collaborate with designers to enhance the app's user experience using UX design tools. Implementing Lean principles, you streamline the development process, ensuring quick iterations and feedback incorporation.

Furthermore, you apply DFSS methodologies to conduct thorough market research, identify customer needs, and design a product that aligns with Six Sigma standards for quality. Throughout the project, Agile methodologies guide your team in responding to changing market demands and delivering incremental updates to the application.

By mastering these advanced tools and methodologies, product managers can navigate complex projects with ease, ensuring successful product launches and satisfying end-user experiences.

Chapter 5: Product Management vs. Project Management

Product management and project management are essential components in the successful delivery of products and projects. Product management involves understanding market demands, identifying opportunities, and creating a roadmap for a successful product launch. On the other hand, project management focuses on overseeing daily tasks, managing resources, and ensuring projects are completed within scope and budget.

In the fast-paced world we live in today, product and project managers play vital roles. Product management covers the entire product lifecycle, from idea to launch and beyond, while project management deals with executing specific tasks within set timeframes and budgets. These roles ensure innovative ideas translate into successful products.

To excel in product and project management, it's crucial to grasp key terms like "roadmap," "backlog," "sprint," and "MVP." A roadmap lays out a product's vision and progress, while the backlog prioritizes features. Sprints are focused work periods, and the MVP is the basic product version for testing.

Effective management requires strategic planning, stakeholder engagement, and risk mitigation. Engaging stakeholders early aligns expectations, while identifying risks early saves time and resources. Agile methodologies enhance flexibility and responsiveness, aiding in adapting to changes swiftly.

Utilizing tools like JIRA, Trello, and Asana streamlines project tracking and team collaboration. Techniques like SWOT analysis offer a comprehensive view of the competitive landscape, and SMART criteria ensure clear goal-setting. Embracing challenges and recognizing successes are vital for personal and team growth.

In conclusion, mastering product and project management involves understanding terminologies, gaining practical insights, and using essential tools. Strengthening skills and embracing challenges lead to success in these dynamic roles. By expanding expertise and refining skills, we navigate the complexities of product management and project management, paving the way for innovation and triumph.

Chapter 6: Product Management vs Product Owner:

In the fast-paced realm of product development, the roles of Product Manager and Product Owner play a pivotal role in shaping a product's journey from inception to the hands of the end-user. These two key positions, though sharing the common goal of delivering outstanding products, bring unique perspectives and responsibilities to the table, combining strategic vision with tactical execution for optimal results.

The Visionary Strategist - Product Manager:

In the realm of product development, the Product Manager assumes the role of a visionary strategist, often likened to the CEO of the product. This position necessitates a strategic approach, with a focus on ensuring the product's long-term success while staying aligned with the overarching vision of the company.

Product Managers act as the bridge between the market and the organization, consistently analysing industry trends, customer demands, and competitive landscapes. They are entrusted with crafting and communicating the product vision, developing and prioritizing the product roadmap, identifying market gaps, and defining key success metrics.

Key Responsibilities of a Product Manager:

- Formulating and articulating the product vision with clarity

- Creating and prioritizing the product roadmap to guide development efforts

- Recognizing market opportunities and addressing customer needs

- Establishing measurable product metrics and success benchmarks

- Collaborating with stakeholders across different departments to ensure alignment

The Agile Executor - Product Owner:

On the flip side, the Product Owner emerges as the agile executor, a role originating from Agile methodologies, notably Scrum. The Product Owner acts as the tactical driving force, translating the strategic vision outlined by the Product Manager into actionable tasks for the development team.

Product Owners closely collaborate with cross-functional teams to guarantee that the product backlog accurately reflects the priorities outlined in the roadmap, ensuring that each sprint delivers tangible value to the end-users. Their responsibilities include managing and prioritizing the product backlog, translating high-level strategies into detailed requirements, working in tandem with development teams during sprints, validating that features meet user expectations and business objectives, and serving as a vital link between the development team and stakeholders.

Synergy and Distinction Between Roles:

While there might be some overlap in responsibilities between Product Managers and Product Owners, their core distinction lies in the scope and focus of their work. Product Managers adopt a strategic, big-picture perspective, while Product Owners are hands-on, ensuring that each product increment aligns with the strategic roadmap.

Trending Skills and Tools to Master:

- Mastery of Agile methodologies for efficient product development

- Embracing user-centric design principles for enhanced user experience

- Facilitating cross-functional collaboration for seamless project execution

- Strategic planning to ensure product success in competitive markets

- Proficiency in product lifecycle management for sustained product relevance

- Nurturing stakeholder consensus for smoother decision-making processes

- Cultivating customer empathy to design products that resonate with users

In conclusion, the Product Manager and Product Owner represent two essential halves of a unified product leadership team, working in harmony to guide products through the ever-evolving landscape of innovation and market demand. Together, they epitomize the blend of strategic foresight and agile execution necessary to not just launch products, but to thrive in the hands of users.

Chapter 7: Mastering Advanced Product Management Tools

Introduction

In the dynamic realm of product management, leveraging cutting-edge tools is crucial for boosting efficiency, streamlining operations, and making informed decisions. This chapter delves into indispensable tools that empower product managers to excel and outlines practical strategies for their effective utilization in real-world projects.

Strategic Road mapping Tools: Envisioning the Path Ahead

Product Plan: A user-friendly platform tailored for crafting visually engaging product roadmaps that align cross-functional teams on strategic goals and monitor progress effectively.

How to Use: Kick off by defining your product's overarching vision and specific objectives. Segment your roadmap into manageable releases and features, allocating timelines and responsibilities to respective teams. Regularly update the roadmap to adapt to evolving priorities and market dynamics.

Aha!: A comprehensive roadmapping solution that seamlessly integrates with diverse project management systems, facilitating seamless ideation capture and meticulous release planning.

How to Use: Develop a strategic blueprint outlining crucial initiatives. Leverage the Ideas portal to collect and prioritize feedback. Construct detailed feature roadmaps that directly tie back to your overarching strategic objectives.

User-Centric Feedback and Testing Tools

UserTesting: An invaluable tool that delivers real-time video feedback from users navigating your product, pinpointing usability pain points and areas ripe for enhancement.

How to Use: Define clear testing objectives and pinpoint your target audience. Craft relevant test scenarios and inquiries, then meticulously analyse recorded sessions to unearth common pain points and enhancement opportunities.

SurveyMonkey: A user-friendly platform for crafting insightful surveys aimed at gathering invaluable customer feedback and insights.

How to Use: Design surveys with concise, pertinent questions focusing on key areas of interest. Disseminate surveys via multiple channels such as email, social media, or in-app prompts. Scrutinize responses to steer product decisions effectively.

Seamless Collaboration and Project Management Tools

Jira: A robust tool tailored for agile project management, bug tracking, and sprint planning.

How to Use: Establish projects and outline user stories or tasks. Leverage sprint planning boards to streamline work organization and prioritization. Monitor progress through detailed reports and fine-tune workflows as needed.

Trello: An intuitive visual project management tool that fosters task and project organization through boards, lists, and cards.

How to Use: Create distinct boards for varied projects or teams. Utilize lists to delineate different workflow stages and cards for individual tasks. Incorporate due dates, labels, and comments for enhanced clarity and accountability.

Data-Driven Analytics and Visualization Tools

Google Analytics: A pivotal tool for deciphering user behaviour on websites or apps, offering valuable insights into traffic patterns, user engagement, and conversion rates.

How to Use: Deploy tracking codes on your website or app. Monitor critical metrics like page views, bounce rates, and user demographics. Utilize these insights to refine product strategies and marketing endeavours.

Tableau: A cutting-edge data visualization tool renowned for crafting interactive and shareable dashboards.

How to Use: Establish connections between Tableau and your data sources. Create captivating visualizations using its intuitive drag-and-drop features. Develop interactive dashboards that empower stakeholders to delve into data and extract actionable insights.

Prototyping and Design Innovation Tools

Figma: A collaborative design powerhouse enabling teams to ideate, prototype, and solicit real-time feedback seamlessly.

How to Use: Build sleek interfaces with Figma's versatile vector tools. Share prototypes with stakeholders for constructive feedback. Leverage Figma's collaborative functionalities to engage in real-time collaboration with team members.

Sketch: A favoured tool among designers for crafting high-fidelity prototypes and sleek interfaces.

How to Use: Create wireframes and prototypes using Sketch's advanced design tools. Harness plugins to augment functionality and enhance workflow efficiency. Share designs with developers for a seamless handover process.

Customer Relationship Management (CRM) Solutions

Salesforce: A robust CRM platform empowering businesses to nurture customer relationships, track sales pipelines, and analyse customer interactions effectively.

How to Use: Tailor Salesforce to align with your unique business processes. Monitor customer interactions, sales funnels, and service cases diligently. Harness analytics to gain deep insights into customer behaviour and sales performance.

HubSpot: An all-encompassing CRM suite offering robust tools for marketing, sales, and customer service operations.

How to Use: Leverage HubSpot's versatile marketing tools to curate and launch impactful campaigns. Monitor customer interactions and deal progressions seamlessly using the sales tools. Deliver exceptional customer service through the support features provided by HubSpot.

Chapter 8: Mastering Real-World Product Management

Introduction

Transitioning from theory to practical application is crucial in mastering product management. This chapter will guide you through the journey from ideation to product release, providing a hands-on sample project to enhance your learning journey.

Unveiling Lucrative Market Opportunities

Explore the market thoroughly to identify profitable gaps and prospects.

Tools of the Trade: Embrace advanced tools like SWOT analysis, competitive analysis, and customer surveys to assess the market landscape effectively.

Crafting a Compelling Product Vision and Strategy

Formulate an engaging product vision that harmonizes with your company's goals.

Strategic Roadmap: Outline essential milestones, resource needs, timelines, unique selling points, and target audience specifics.

Plotting the Product Journey

Utilize state-of-the-art roadmapping tools to visualize your product's progression from concept to realization.

Practical Implementation: Break down the roadmap into manageable phases, delegate tasks, and set realistic deadlines. Regularly updating the roadmap is vital for adapting to dynamic changes.

Developing the MVP (Minimum Viable Product)

Focus on building a product with key features to attract early users and gather feedback.

Feature Prioritization: Leverage frameworks like Moscow to prioritize features efficiently.

User-Centric Testing and Refinement

Participate in user testing sessions to gather valuable insights.

Iterative Approach: Analyse feedback, identify common pain points, and make necessary improvements. Repeat this cycle until the product meets user expectations.

Executing a Successful Product Launch

Create a comprehensive go-to-market strategy encompassing marketing and sales tactics.

Launch Tactics: Collaborate with cross-functional teams for a smooth launch. Stay attentive to initial user feedback and address any issues promptly.

Post-Launch Enhancement Strategies

Monitor key performance indicators (KPIs) to assess product performance.

Continuous Improvement: Collect user feedback, incorporate enhancements, and schedule regular updates based on user needs and market trends.

Advanced Trending Tools for Product Management:

1. Airtable: A versatile tool for organizing and collaborating on product development tasks.

2. Mixpanel: Enables deep user analytics to optimize product performance.

3. Miro: Facilitates visual collaboration for product planning and brainstorming.

4. Notion: A comprehensive workspace for project management and documentation.

5. Product board: Helps streamline product management processes and prioritize features effectively.

By integrating these advanced tools into your workflow, you can elevate your skills and transition from a novice to a proficient product management professional.

Sample Project: Crafting a New Mobile Fitness App

Step 1: Market Exploration

- Objective: Identify a niche market for a fitness tracking app tailored to busy professionals.

- Actions: Conduct surveys, interviews, and competitor analysis to pinpoint market needs and preferences.

Step 2: Vision and Strategy Development

- Vision: "Empowering busy professionals to achieve fitness goals through personalized and convenient tracking."

- Strategy: Emphasize features like quick workout logging, wearable device integration, and personalized fitness plans.

Step 3: Roadmapping Tool

- Tool: Leverage ProductPlan for creating a detailed roadmap with key features, development phases, and launch timelines.

Step 4: MVP Development

- Core Features: Workout logging, device integration, and basic fitness plans.

- Tool: Opt for Trello for streamlined task management to ensure on-time delivery.

Step 5: User Testing and Refinement

- Tool: Utilize UserTesting for comprehensive user feedback sessions.

- Actions: Analyse insights, address common issues, and refine the app for an enhanced user experience.

Step 6: Product Launch

- Strategy: Execute a robust go-to-market strategy leveraging social media and partnerships with fitness influencers.

- Coordination: Collaborate with the marketing team to craft compelling promotional materials and campaigns.

Step 7: Post-Launch Monitoring

- Analytics: Utilize Google Analytics to track app usage and user engagement.

- Feedback Loop: Continuously gather user feedback and enhance the app to meet evolving user needs.

Conclusion

Mastering advanced tools and integrating them into real-world projects is pivotal for successful product management. By embracing these tools and following a structured approach, you can elevate your skills and drive your product towards triumph.

Chapter 9: Mastering Real-World Product Management Challenges

Introduction

Product Management Mastery in Today's Ever-Changing World

In the fast-paced realm of product management, a profound grasp of cutting-edge tools and strategies is essential for conquering obstacles and achieving triumph. This chapter is your gateway to navigating real-world challenges with finesse.

Unleashing the Power of Stakeholder Relations

- Masterful Communication: Elevate stakeholder interactions through transparent communication, timely updates, and setting realistic goals.

- Tools of the Trade: Harness the potential of collaborative platforms like Slack or Microsoft Teams for seamless communication and alignment.

Embracing Market Dynamics with Agility

- Flexibility at its Finest: Embrace adaptability to swiftly respond to market shifts and evolving trends.

- State-of-the-Art Tools: Utilize advanced data analytics tools such as Mixpanel for real-time monitoring of market trends and user behaviour.

Balancing Innovation and Practicality

- Cultivating Creativity: Empower your team to think outside the box and experiment boldly.

- Innovation with Purpose: Ensure innovative solutions are not just revolutionary but also feasible and in line with business objectives.

- Tools of Innovation: Utilize idea management platforms like Brightidea to capture, assess, and nurture groundbreaking concepts.

Promoting Seamless Cross-Functional Collaboration

- Nurturing Strong Team Dynamics: Foster a collaborative environment built on teamwork and mutual respect.

- Vital Collaboration Tools: Enhance teamwork efficiency with project management applications like Asana or Monday.com for seamless task coordination across departments.

Strategic Feature Prioritization and Resource Allocation

- Strategic Decision-Making: Implement prioritization frameworks like RICE (Reach, Impact, Confidence, Effort) for data-driven decision-making.

- Key Tools for Success: Optimize feature prioritization using product management tools such as Airfocus to visualize and rank features effectively.

In Conclusion

Mastering the art of product management in the real world requires a blend of strategic prowess, effective communication, and leveraging cutting-edge tools. By embracing these strategies, product managers can confidently navigate challenges, ensuring product success in today's competitive landscape.

Chapter 10: Advanced Techniques for Data-Driven Product Management

Introduction

In the ever-changing world of product management, mastering data-driven decision-making is crucial for achieving success. This chapter explores the latest methods for gathering, analysing, and leveraging data to shape product strategies and enhance user experiences, making it an exciting and easy-to-understand journey.

Crafting a strategic roadmap for the evolution of data insights involves understanding the journey from basic to advanced levels. Advanced data collection strategies go beyond the basics by diving into predictive modelling and other advanced analytics to predict user behaviour trends. Delving deeper with qualitative data involves exploring immersive techniques such as eye-tracking studies and sentiment analysis for richer insights. Sophisticated data analysis techniques include real-time data visualization and machine learning enhancements for dynamic data visualization and personalized user recommendations.

Data-driven decision-making in action includes employing advanced recommendation algorithms for dynamic feature prioritization and hyper-personalized customer segmentation. Crafting strategic data-driven roadmaps involves utilizing AI-driven roadmap optimization tools to adjust product roadmaps dynamically based on real-time data and market trends, as well as implementing agile data validation methodologies for continuous validation of product assumptions through rapid experimentation.

Measuring product success with precision entails developing customized KPI frameworks integrating advanced metrics for comprehensive performance assessment and implementing AI-driven predictive analytics tools for forecasting product performance trends.

Conclusion

In the dynamic field of product management, mastering advanced data-driven techniques is the gateway to unlocking unparalleled insights and achieving remarkable success. By adopting cutting-edge tools and methodologies, product managers can confidently navigate challenges and deliver exceptional products that truly resonate with users.

Chapter 11: Advanced Agile Product Management

Introduction

Agile methodologies have revolutionized product development and management in recent years. This chapter delves deeper into Agile practices, providing insights on practical applications in product management.

Agile Core Concepts:

- Principles: Agile emphasizes customer collaboration, flexibility, and iterative progress. It prioritizes individuals and interactions over processes and tools, working software over comprehensive documentation, customer collaboration over contract negotiation, and responding to change over following a plan.

- Manifesto: The Agile Manifesto outlines the core values and principles of Agile, emphasizing adaptability and a customer-centric approach.

Scrum Framework:

- **Key Roles:**

- o Product Owner: Shapes the product backlog and prioritizes requirements.
- o Scrum Master: Guides the team in following Agile practices.
- o Development Team: Executes tasks and delivers product increments.

- **Essential Ceremonies:**
  - o Sprint Planning: Collaboratively plan work for the upcoming sprint.
  - o Daily Stand-Ups: Brief meetings for synchronization and issue identification.
  - o Sprint Reviews: Showcasing work to stakeholders at sprint completion.
  - o Sprint Retrospectives: Reflecting on the sprint for continuous improvement.

- **Vital Artifacts:**
  - o Product Backlog: Prioritized features and tasks list.
  - o Sprint Backlog: Subset of product backlog items for the sprint.

- o Increment: Working product delivered at the end of each sprint.

Kanban Method:

- Core Principles: Kanban stresses work visualization, limiting work in progress (WIP), and enhancing flow efficiency.

- Board Configuration: Utilize columns like "To Do," "In Progress," and "Done" to manage tasks.

Practical Application of Agile in Product Management:

- Backlog Refinement: Continuously refine and prioritize the product backlog to adapt to changing requirements.

- Sprint Goal Setting: Define clear objectives and tasks for each sprint in alignment with the product strategy.

- User-Centric Approach: Craft user stories using the format: "As a [user], I want [feature] so that [benefit]."

Agile Performance Measurement:

- Key Metrics: Monitor velocity, burndown charts, and cycle time to track progress effectively.

- Feedback Integration: Regularly seek feedback from users and stakeholders for product enhancement.

Overcoming Challenges:

- Agile Scaling: Implement frameworks like Safe for managing Agile practices in larger organizations.

- Managing Distributed Teams: Effective communication tools are essential for coordinating remote Agile teams.

Agile methodologies offer a dynamic and iterative product management approach. By embracing Agile principles, product managers can swiftly adapt to changes, foster collaboration, and deliver top-notch products efficiently.

Sample Project: Developing a Task Management Application using Agile Principles

In this project, a team of developers, guided by a Product Owner and Scrum Master, will utilize Agile methodologies to create a task management application. The project will involve defining user stories, sprint planning, iterative development, and continuous feedback integration to deliver a functional product.

Chapter 12: Innovative Strategies for Product Development

Introduction

Innovation plays a crucial role in maintaining competitiveness in today's market landscape. This chapter explores strategies and tools for fostering innovation in product development.

Cultivating an Innovation Culture

- Stimulating Creativity: Create an environment that encourages idea sharing and innovation. Recognize and reward innovative thinking.

- Innovation Initiatives: Implement programs like hackathons and innovation labs to drive creativity.

Ideation Approaches

- Brainstorming Sessions: Conduct collaborative idea generation sessions. Utilize techniques such as mind mapping for diverse perspectives.

- Design Thinking: Empathize with users, define problems, ideate solutions, prototype, and test for innovative outcomes.

Prototyping and User Testing

- Rapid Prototyping: Quickly build and test prototypes to validate ideas and gather feedback.

  - Tools: Figma and Invision facilitate interactive prototype creation.

- User-Centric Testing: Gather insights from real users to refine concepts and meet user needs effectively.

  - Tools: User Testing and Usability Hub aid in conducting user testing sessions.

Innovation Frameworks

- Lean Startup Methodology: Focus on building MVPs, measuring results, and learning iteratively from feedback.

- Jobs to Be Done (JTBD) Framework: Design products based on understanding customer needs and solving their problems.

- Blue Ocean Strategy: Identify new market spaces for innovative product creation.

Scaling Innovation Efforts

- Concept to Product Transition: Streamline processes and promote cross-functional collaboration for successful product development.

- Innovation Portfolio Management: Balance incremental and disruptive innovations to mitigate risks and drive growth.

Conclusion

Innovation is the cornerstone of market growth and differentiation. By fostering an innovative culture and leveraging effective ideation and prototyping strategies, product managers can drive forward groundbreaking products that meet evolving customer demands.

Chapter 13: Advanced Leadership Strategies for Product Managers

Introduction

In the fast-paced world of product management, mastering advanced leadership skills is crucial for driving innovation and guiding teams towards success. This chapter delves into practical and cutting-edge leadership principles tailored specifically for product managers.

Visionary Leadership Reinvented

- Crafting a Vision: Elevate your vision creation process by incorporating AI-driven market analysis and predictive modelling to anticipate future trends and customer needs.

- Inspiring Teams: Transform your storytelling approach by integrating immersive virtual reality experiences to engage and motivate your team like never before.

Influence and Persuasion Mastery

- Stakeholder Management: Utilize advanced stakeholder mapping tools to visualize and prioritize key relationships, ensuring alignment with strategic objectives.

- Communication Skills: Harness the power of AI-powered language processing tools to tailor communication styles dynamically based on real-time audience feedback.

Decision-Making in the Digital Age

- Data-Driven Decisions: Implement machine learning algorithms to analyse complex datasets and extract actionable insights for more precise decision-making.

- Balancing Risk and Reward: Utilize scenario planning software to simulate various outcomes and optimize risk management strategies effectively.

Conflict Resolution Excellence

- Identifying Conflicts: Employ sentiment analysis tools to proactively detect potential conflicts within teams or with stakeholders, enabling swift resolution.

- Mediation Techniques: Implement virtual reality conflict resolution simulations to enhance empathy and communication skills among team members.

Revolutionary Team Building Techniques

- Hiring the Right Talent: Leverage AI-driven talent acquisition platforms to identify candidates with the perfect blend of skills, cultural fit, and passion for the product.

- Fostering Collaboration: Utilize collaborative virtual workspaces powered by augmented reality to facilitate seamless cross-functional teamwork and ideation.

Continuous Learning in the Digital Era

- Professional Development Redefined: Explore virtual reality training modules and gamified learning experiences to upskill yourself and your team in an engaging and interactive manner.

- Feedback Loops Reinvented: Implement AI-powered feedback analytics tools to gather, analyse, and act upon feedback from multiple sources efficiently.

Conclusion

Embracing advanced leadership strategies is the key to unlocking the full potential of product management in today's dynamic landscape. By embracing innovative tools and techniques, product managers can inspire their teams, make informed decisions, and propel their products to new heights.

Sample Project: AI-Powered Product Vision Simulator

In this project, you will develop an AI-powered tool that analyses market trends, customer feedback, and competitor strategies to generate a futuristic product vision. By incorporating machine learning algorithms and natural language processing capabilities, the tool will help product managers craft compelling visions aligned with evolving market demands.

Chapter 14: Elevating Remote Product Team Management

Introduction

The shift towards remote work has revolutionized the way product teams collaborate and innovate. This chapter explores advanced strategies and tools for effectively leading remote product teams in a rapidly evolving digital landscape.

Next-Level Communication Tactics

- Real-Time Collaboration: Embrace AI-powered virtual collaboration platforms that facilitate seamless communication and brainstorming sessions across distributed teams.

  - Tools: Integrate cutting-edge tools like Spatial and Miro for immersive collaborative experiences.

Cultivating Trust in Virtual Environments

- Virtual Team Building Innovations: Implement virtual reality team-building exercises and immersive experiences to strengthen team bonds and foster a sense of belonging.

- Transparent Practices Redefined: Utilize blockchain technology to ensure transparency and accountability in remote team operations.

Productivity Enhancement Strategies

- Agile Remote Workflows: Implement AI-driven project management systems that enhance team productivity and streamline remote collaboration.

  - Tools: Embrace advanced platforms such as Monday.com and Click Up for efficient task management and progress tracking.

Overcoming Global Challenges with Technology

- Time Zone Optimization: Utilize smart scheduling algorithms and AI assistants to coordinate meetings and optimize work schedules across different time zones.

- Cultural Intelligence Solutions: Leverage AI-based cultural sensitivity training modules to promote inclusivity and cross-cultural understanding within remote teams.

Performance Excellence in Virtual Settings

- Continuous Feedback Mechanisms: Implement real-time feedback tools powered by machine learning to provide personalized performance insights and development suggestions.

- Recognition Automation: Integrate AI-driven recognition systems to acknowledge and reward team achievements in a timely and impactful manner.

Conclusion

Empowering remote product teams with advanced technologies and innovative practices is essential for driving collaboration, productivity, and success in the digital age. By embracing cutting-edge tools and strategies, product managers can lead their distributed teams to achieve exceptional results.

Chapter 16: Interview Preparation Questions and Answers for Product Managers and Designers

Introduction

Preparing for interviews is essential for aspiring product managers and designers. This chapter provides a comprehensive guide with sample questions and answers to help you succeed in your interviews. This chapter provides questions and answers that are commonly asked in product management and product design interviews. These examples will help you articulate your experiences and showcase your skills effectively.

Sample Questions and Answers for Product Managers

1. How do you stay current with industry trends and market changes?

   Answer: "I stay current by regularly reading industry blogs, following thought leaders on social media, and participating in webinars and conferences. I also engage with professional networks and attend meetups to discuss trends and innovations with peers. Subscribing to newsletters and being active in relevant online communities helps me keep a pulse on market changes and emerging technologies."

2. Describe a time when you had to pivot a product strategy. What was the outcome?

   Answer: "At my previous job, we initially launched a product aimed at small businesses, but it didn't gain the traction we anticipated. After analysing user feedback and market data, we discovered a significant demand from mid-sized enterprises. We decided to pivot our strategy, updating our features and marketing approach to better serve this new target audience. This pivot resulted in a 50% increase in user acquisition and significantly improved customer satisfaction."

3. How do you handle feature requests from stakeholders?

   Answer: "I handle feature requests by first understanding the underlying need or problem the stakeholder is addressing. I then evaluate the request against our current roadmap, business objectives, and user feedback. I use a prioritization framework like RICE to assess the impact and feasibility of the request. If the request aligns with our goals and adds value, I incorporate it into our backlog. If not, I communicate the reasoning and provide alternative solutions if possible."

4. What is your approach to managing product launches?

   Answer: "My approach to managing product launches involves detailed planning and coordination. I start by creating a launch plan that outlines key milestones, timelines, and responsibilities. I ensure thorough testing and quality assurance to deliver a reliable product. Collaborating with marketing, sales, and customer support teams is crucial for a smooth launch. Post-launch, I monitor performance metrics and gather user feedback to address any issues and plan future iterations."

5. Can you explain a time when you had to make a difficult trade-off decision?

   Answer: "In a previous project, we had limited resources and had to choose between implementing a highly requested feature and improving the existing user interface. After conducting a user survey and analysing usage data, I decided to prioritize the user interface improvements because it would enhance the overall user experience and benefit a larger portion of our users. While some stakeholders were initially disappointed, the decision ultimately led to increased user satisfaction and engagement."

6. How do you handle a product that is not meeting performance expectations?

   Answer: "When a product is not meeting performance expectations, I start by diagnosing the root cause. I analyse key metrics, user feedback, and market data to identify issues. I then convene a cross-functional team to brainstorm solutions and prioritize actions based on impact and feasibility. We might iterate on features, adjust our marketing strategy, or even pivot the product if necessary. Continuous monitoring and agile iterations help us improve the product's performance over time."

7. Describe your experience with setting and measuring OKRs (Objectives and Key Results).

Answer: "In my previous role, I was responsible for setting quarterly OKRs for my product team. We started by aligning our objectives with the company's strategic goals. Each objective was specific, measurable, and ambitious. For example, one objective was to increase user engagement, with key results focused on metrics like daily active users and session duration. We regularly reviewed progress in team meetings and adjusted our tactics as needed. This framework helped us stay focused and drive meaningful results."

8. How do you manage technical debt while continuously delivering new features?

   Answer: "Managing technical debt requires balancing immediate needs with long-term sustainability. I work closely with engineering to identify and prioritize technical debt issues alongside new feature development. We allocate a portion of each sprint to address high-priority technical debt. This prevents it from accumulating and ensures our codebase remains maintainable. Regularly reviewing and refactoring code, combined with automated testing, helps us manage technical debt effectively without compromising on feature delivery."

9. Can you describe a situation where you had to influence a decision without direct authority?

Answer: "In one project, I needed to persuade the marketing team to shift their campaign strategy to better align with our product's value proposition. I gathered data from user research and market analysis to build a compelling case. I presented my findings in a meeting, highlighting how the proposed changes could drive better user engagement and conversion rates. By focusing on data-driven insights and aligning our goals, I was able to influence their decision and implement a more effective strategy."

10. How do you approach building a product roadmap?

Answer: "Building a product roadmap involves several key steps. First, I gather input from stakeholders, including customer feedback, market trends, and business objectives. I prioritize initiatives using frameworks like MoSCoW or RICE. The roadmap is then structured to reflect short-term and long-term goals, with clear timelines and milestones. I ensure it remains flexible to adapt to changing circumstances. Regularly reviewing and updating the roadmap with the team ensures alignment and keeps everyone informed."

11. What is your approach to managing a product's lifecycle from inception to retirement?

Answer: "Managing a product's lifecycle involves several stages: inception, development, growth, maturity, and retirement. During inception, I focus on market research and feasibility studies. In development, I work closely with engineering and design teams to build the product. Growth involves scaling and optimizing for user acquisition and retention. Maturity requires sustaining market share and iterating based on feedback. Finally, in the retirement stage, I plan for a smooth transition, ensuring support for users and migrating them to alternative solutions if needed."

12. How do you handle competing priorities and ensure alignment across teams?

Answer: "I handle competing priorities by clearly defining goals and using a prioritization framework like

RICE (Reach, Impact, Confidence, Effort). Regular communication with stakeholders helps ensure alignment. I facilitate cross-functional meetings to discuss priorities and make data-driven decisions. By keeping everyone informed and focusing on the most impactful tasks, I ensure the team stays aligned and works efficiently."

13. Describe a situation where you had to make a data-driven decision.

Answer: "In a previous role, we noticed a drop in user engagement on our platform. I analysed user data to identify patterns and pinpointed the issue to a specific feature. By conducting A/B tests and gathering user feedback, we discovered that the feature was not intuitive. I proposed a redesign, which we implemented and tested. The data showed a significant improvement in user engagement, validating our decision."

14. How do you approach market analysis for a new product?

Answer: "Market analysis for a new product starts with identifying the target market and understanding customer needs. I conduct SWOT (Strengths, Weaknesses, Opportunities, Threats) analysis, competitive analysis, and market segmentation. Gathering data from primary sources like surveys and interviews, as well as secondary sources like industry reports, provides comprehensive insights. This analysis helps in shaping the product strategy and positioning."

15. What metrics do you use to measure product success and why?

    Answer: "The metrics I use depend on the product and its goals. Common metrics include user engagement (daily active users, session duration), customer satisfaction (NPS scores), retention rates, and revenue growth. For a SaaS product, I might focus on MRR (Monthly Recurring Revenue) and churn rate. These metrics provide a holistic view of the product's performance and help in making informed decisions."

16. How do you foster innovation within your team?

    Answer: "Fostering innovation involves creating an environment that encourages creativity and experimentation. I encourage open communication and idea-sharing through regular brainstorming sessions. Providing time and resources for experimentation, such as hackathons or innovation sprints, helps the team explore new ideas. Recognizing and rewarding innovative contributions also motivates the team to think outside the box."

17. Can you discuss a time when you had to pivot a product strategy based on user feedback?

Answer: "At one point, we launched a new feature that didn't resonate well with users. Through user feedback and analytics, we identified the shortcomings. We quickly pivoted our strategy by addressing the feedback, simplifying the feature, and improving its usability. This pivot required coordination with multiple teams, but the improved feature was well-received, leading to increased user satisfaction and engagement."

18. How do you manage stakeholder expectations during a product development cycle?

Answer: "Managing stakeholder expectations involves clear communication and setting realistic goals. I keep stakeholders informed through regular updates and transparent reporting. Setting milestones and providing early prototypes or demos helps manage expectations. I also ensure stakeholders are involved in key decisions, which builds trust and keeps everyone aligned."

19. What is your approach to competitive analysis?

Answer: "My approach to competitive analysis involves identifying key competitors and analysing their strengths and weaknesses. I study their product features, pricing, market positioning, and customer reviews. Tools like SWOT analysis help in understanding where we stand relative to competitors. This analysis informs our product strategy, highlighting opportunities for differentiation and areas where we need to improve."

20. How do you prioritize technical debt against new features?

Answer: "Prioritizing technical debt involves balancing short-term and long-term goals. I work with the engineering team to assess the impact of technical debt on product performance and development speed. We allocate a portion of each sprint to address critical technical debt issues. This approach prevents technical debt from accumulating and ensures that new features can be delivered efficiently."

21. Describe your experience with agile methodologies.

Answer: "I have extensive experience with agile methodologies, including Scrum and Kanban. I use agile principles to promote iterative development and continuous improvement. In Scrum, I facilitate sprint planning, daily stand-ups, sprint reviews, and retrospectives. Kanban helps visualize workflow and manage ongoing tasks. Agile methodologies enhance team collaboration, adaptability, and transparency, leading to better product outcomes."

22. How do you handle a product failure?

Answer: "Handling a product failure involves analysing what went wrong and learning from the experience. I start by conducting a thorough post-mortem analysis to identify the root causes. Gathering feedback from users and team members provides valuable insights. Based on the findings, I implement changes to prevent similar issues in the future. Communicating transparently with stakeholders and focusing on continuous improvement helps turn failure into a learning opportunity."

23. What is your approach to user onboarding?

Answer: "Effective user onboarding involves creating a seamless and intuitive experience that helps users understand the product's value quickly. I design onboarding flows that guide users through key features step-by-step. Using tutorials, tooltips, and interactive walkthroughs enhances the onboarding process. Collecting user feedback and analysing engagement metrics helps refine and optimize the onboarding experience."

24. How do you balance long-term vision with short-term goals?

Answer: "Balancing long-term vision with short-term goals requires clear prioritization and strategic planning. I create a product roadmap that outlines long-term objectives and breaks them down into achievable short-term goals. Regularly reviewing and adjusting the roadmap ensures we stay aligned with the vision while meeting immediate needs. This approach maintains focus on the big picture while delivering incremental value."

25.What strategies do you use for go-to-market planning?

Answer: "Go-to-market planning involves defining the target audience, crafting messaging, and coordinating with sales and marketing teams. I start by conducting market research to understand customer needs and competitive landscape. Developing a value proposition and positioning statement helps communicate the product's benefits. I work closely with marketing to create promotional materials and with sales to train them on the product. Setting clear goals and KPIs ensures we can measure the success of the launch."

26.How do you incorporate user feedback into product development?

Answer: "Incorporating user feedback involves gathering insights through surveys, interviews, and usability tests. I prioritize feedback based on its impact on user experience and alignment with our goals. Creating user stories and incorporating them into the product backlog ensures feedback is actionable.

Continuous iteration and regular communication with users help validate changes and improve the product."

27. Describe a time when you had to manage a product with a limited budget.

Answer: "Managing a product with a limited budget requires prioritizing features that deliver the most value. In one project, we had a tight budget and had to focus on core functionalities. I conducted a thorough cost-benefit analysis and engaged with stakeholders to align on priorities. By leveraging open-source tools and optimizing resource allocation, we successfully delivered a product that met user needs and business goals within budget constraints."

28. How do you ensure cross-functional team alignment?

Answer: "Ensuring cross-functional team alignment involves clear communication and collaborative planning. I facilitate regular meetings to discuss goals, progress, and challenges. Using tools like shared roadmaps and project management software helps keep everyone on the same page. Encouraging open dialogue and fostering a culture of collaboration ensures all teams work towards common objectives."

29. What is your approach to risk management in product development?

Answer: "Risk management involves identifying, assessing, and mitigating potential risks throughout the product development cycle. I start by conducting a risk assessment to identify possible issues. Prioritizing risks based on their impact and likelihood helps focus on critical areas. Developing contingency plans and regularly reviewing risks with the team ensures we are prepared to address any challenges that arise."

30. How do you handle product localization for different markets?

Answer: "Product localization involves adapting the product to meet the cultural, linguistic, and regulatory requirements of different markets. I start by conducting market research to understand the local needs and preferences. Collaborating with local experts and translators ensures accuracy and relevance. Implementing flexible design and architecture allows for easy adaptation. Continuous testing and feedback from local users help refine and improve the localized product."

31. What methods do you use for user segmentation?

Answer: "User segmentation involves dividing users into distinct groups based on common characteristics. I use methods like demographic segmentation, behavioural segmentation, and psychographic segmentation. Analysing user data helps identify patterns and create segments. This approach allows for targeted marketing and personalized user experiences, improving engagement and satisfaction."

32. How do you prioritize features when resources are constrained?

Answer: "When resources are constrained, I prioritize features based on their impact on user experience and business goals. Using frameworks like Moscow (Must-have, Should-have, Could-have, Won't-have) helps categorize features. Engaging with stakeholders and users to gather input ensures we focus on the most valuable features. This approach maximizes resource efficiency while delivering meaningful product improvements."

33. Describe your experience with conducting user research.

Answer: "I have extensive experience conducting user research, including interviews, surveys, and usability tests. I start by defining research objectives and selecting appropriate methods. Gathering qualitative and quantitative data provides comprehensive insights. Analysing the data helps identify user needs, pain points, and opportunities for improvement. Integrating these insights into the product development process ensures we create user-cantered solutions."

34. How do you manage remote teams and ensure productivity?

Answer: "Managing remote teams involves clear communication, regular check-ins, and leveraging collaboration tools. I establish clear expectations and provide regular updates to keep everyone aligned. Tools like Slack, Zoom, and project management software help facilitate communication and collaboration.

Encouraging a healthy work-life balance and fostering a sense of team culture ensures productivity and engagement."

35. How do you handle a situation where the team is not meeting deadlines?

Answer: "When the team is not meeting deadlines, I start by identifying the root causes. Engaging with team members to understand their challenges provides valuable insights. Adjusting the project plan, reallocating resources, or providing additional support can help address the issues. Regularly reviewing progress and setting realistic milestones ensures we stay on track. Open communication and fostering a collaborative environment help the team overcome obstacles and meet deadlines."

36. What is your approach to conducting A/B tests?

Answer: "Conducting A/B tests involves defining clear hypotheses and selecting appropriate metrics. I create variations of the feature or design and split the user base randomly to test each version. Monitoring performance data helps determine which variation performs better. Analysing the results provides insights into user preferences and informs future decisions. Continuous testing and iteration ensure we optimize the product for the best user experience."

37. How do you integrate data analytics into product management?

Answer: "Integrating data analytics involves using data to inform decision-making throughout the product lifecycle. I use analytics tools to track key metrics and gather insights on user behaviour. Regularly reviewing data helps identify trends, opportunities, and areas for improvement. Collaborating with data analysts and leveraging dashboards ensures data-driven decisions. This approach enhances product performance and aligns with business goals."

38. Describe a time when you had to manage a product launch under tight deadlines.

Answer: "Managing a product launch under tight deadlines requires meticulous planning and coordination. In one project, we faced a tight deadline due to market opportunities. I created a detailed launch plan with clear milestones and responsibilities. Regular check-ins and close collaboration with cross-functional teams ensured we stayed on track. Despite the tight timeline, we successfully launched the product on schedule, meeting our targets and receiving positive feedback."

39. How do you ensure your product is compliant with regulations and standards?

Answer: "Ensuring compliance with regulations and standards involves staying informed about relevant laws and industry standards. I collaborate with legal and compliance teams to understand requirements. Conducting regular audits and incorporating compliance checks into the development process helps identify and address issues early. Providing training and resources for the team ensures everyone is aware of compliance obligations. This proactive approach minimizes risks and ensures regulatory adherence."

40. What is your approach to handling customer complaints and feedback?

Answer: "Handling customer complaints and feedback involves listening, empathizing, and taking action. I ensure customer support channels are easily accessible and responsive. Gathering feedback through surveys, reviews, and direct interactions provides valuable insights. Prioritizing and addressing common issues helps improve the product. Regularly communicating with customers and providing updates on resolutions builds trust and enhances satisfaction."

41. Describe a time when you had to balance innovation with existing product stability.

Answer: "Balancing innovation with product stability requires careful planning and risk management. In one project, we wanted to introduce innovative features while maintaining stability. I created a phased rollout plan, starting with a small user segment to test new features. Continuous monitoring and gathering feedback ensured stability was not compromised. Gradually expanding the rollout allowed us to innovate while maintaining a reliable product."

42. How do you ensure continuous improvement in your product?

Answer: "Continuous improvement involves regularly evaluating and iterating on the product. I gather user feedback, analyse performance metrics, and conduct usability tests to identify areas for improvement. Implementing agile methodologies and fostering a culture of experimentation encourages continuous iteration. Setting clear goals and measuring progress ensures we make consistent enhancements that add value to users."

43. What is your approach to creating a product vision?

Answer: "Creating a product vision involves understanding market needs, user pain points, and business goals. I conduct thorough research and engage with stakeholders to gather insights. Crafting a clear and compelling vision statement that articulates the product's purpose and value helps align the team. Regularly communicating and revisiting the vision ensures it remains relevant and guides strategic decisions."

44. How do you manage dependencies between multiple products or projects?

Answer: "Managing dependencies involves clear planning and coordination. I use tools like Gantt charts and project management software to map out dependencies and timelines. Regularly communicating with teams and stakeholders helps identify potential conflicts and address them proactively. Setting clear priorities and aligning on shared goals ensures smooth execution and minimizes risks."

45. Describe a situation where you had to influence senior management to adopt your product strategy.

Answer: "In one project, I needed senior management to approve a strategic pivot. I prepared a detailed presentation with market data, user insights, and projected outcomes. Highlighting the benefits and potential risks of not adopting the strategy helped build a compelling case. Engaging in open discussions and addressing their concerns ensured alignment. Ultimately, senior management approved the strategy, leading to successful implementation and positive results."

46. How do you handle scope creep in a project?

Answer: "Handling scope creep involves setting clear boundaries and managing expectations. I start by defining and documenting project scope and requirements. Regularly reviewing progress and conducting scope checks helps identify deviations early. Communicating with stakeholders and making data-driven decisions ensures we stay focused on priorities. If changes are necessary, I assess their impact and adjust plans accordingly to minimize disruption."

47. What is your approach to fostering a user-centric culture within your team?

Answer: "Fostering a user-centric culture involves emphasizing the importance of user needs and feedback. I encourage the team to engage with users through interviews, surveys, and usability tests. Sharing user stories and insights regularly keeps the team focused on the user experience. Recognizing and rewarding efforts that prioritize user needs reinforces the culture. This approach ensures we build products that truly resonate with our users."

48. How do you stay motivated and keep your team motivated during challenging times?

Answer: "Staying motivated involves maintaining a positive attitude and focusing on the bigger picture. I keep the team motivated by providing clear goals, regular feedback, and recognizing their achievements. Creating a supportive and collaborative environment helps everyone stay engaged. During challenging times, open communication and encouraging a problem-solving mindset help us overcome obstacles together."

49. Describe your experience with integrating third-party tools or services into your product.

Answer: "Integrating third-party tools involves careful planning and collaboration. In one project, we integrated a third-party payment gateway. I worked closely with the vendor to understand their API and integration requirements. Conducting thorough testing and collaborating with the engineering team ensured a smooth implementation. Continuous monitoring and maintaining clear documentation helped address any issues promptly."

50. How do you handle a situation where market conditions change rapidly?

Answer: "Handling rapid market changes involves staying informed and adaptable. I regularly monitor market trends and gather competitive intelligence. If conditions change, I quickly assess the impact and adjust our strategy accordingly. Engaging with stakeholders and the team to realign on priorities ensures we can respond effectively. Flexibility and proactive planning help us navigate uncertainties and seize new opportunities."

51. What is your approach to developing a product pricing strategy?

Answer: "Developing a pricing strategy involves understanding the market, competition, and customer willingness to pay. I conduct market research and analyse pricing models used by competitors. Gathering feedback through surveys and interviews helps understand customer perceptions of value. Using cost-plus pricing, value-based pricing, or competitive pricing strategies, I develop a pricing model that aligns with our business goals and market positioning."

52. Describe a time when you had to make a tough decision with incomplete information.

Answer: "In a previous role, we faced a situation where we had to decide on a feature release with incomplete user data. I gathered as much information as possible and consulted with the team and stakeholders. We assessed the potential risks and benefits, made an informed decision, and closely monitored the outcome. The decision turned out to be beneficial, and we iterated based on subsequent feedback. Being decisive and adaptive helped us move forward effectively."

53. How do you handle disagreements with stakeholders?

Answer: "Handling disagreements involves active listening, empathy, and finding common ground. I start by understanding the stakeholder's perspective and concerns. Providing data-driven insights and aligning on shared goals helps build a case for my position. If disagreements persist, I seek to compromise and find a mutually beneficial solution. Maintaining open communication and building strong relationships ensures we can navigate conflicts constructively."

54. What is your approach to defining product requirements?

Answer: "Defining product requirements involves gathering inputs from users, stakeholders, and market research. I start by creating user stories and personas to understand needs and pain points. Collaborating with cross-functional teams helps refine and prioritize requirements. Documenting clear and detailed requirements ensures alignment and guides the development process. Regularly reviewing and updating requirements based on feedback and progress ensures they remain relevant."

55. How do you ensure your product stays ahead of the competition?

Answer: "Staying ahead of the competition involves continuous innovation and market awareness. I regularly conduct competitive analysis to understand their strengths and weaknesses. Gathering user feedback and monitoring industry trends helps identify opportunities for differentiation. Fostering a culture of innovation within the team ensures we explore new ideas and stay agile. By continuously iterating and improving, we can maintain a competitive edge."

56. Describe your experience with roadmap planning.

Answer: "Roadmap planning involves setting strategic goals and aligning them with timelines and resources. I start by defining the product vision and key objectives. Engaging with stakeholders and the team helps prioritize features and initiatives. Creating a visual roadmap that outlines milestones and dependencies ensures clarity and alignment. Regularly reviewing and updating the roadmap based on progress and market changes ensures it remains relevant and actionable."

57. How do you approach managing product scalability?

Answer: "Managing product scalability involves planning for growth and optimizing performance. I work closely with the engineering team to design scalable architecture and infrastructure. Conducting load testing and performance monitoring helps identify bottlenecks and areas for improvement. Implementing best practices for coding, database management, and cloud services ensures the product can handle increased usage. Regularly reviewing and updating the scalability plan ensures we are prepared for growth."

58. How do you incorporate sustainability into product management?

Answer: "Incorporating sustainability involves considering environmental and social impacts throughout the product lifecycle. I start by assessing the sustainability of materials, processes, and suppliers. Implementing eco-friendly design principles and promoting energy efficiency helps reduce environmental impact. Engaging with stakeholders and users to understand their sustainability expectations informs our strategy. Regularly reviewing and improving our practices ensures we contribute positively to sustainability goals."

59. What is your approach to handling negative user feedback?

Answer: "Handling negative user feedback involves listening, empathizing, and taking action. I ensure feedback channels are easily accessible and responsive. Analysing feedback to identify common issues and root causes helps prioritize improvements. Communicating transparently with users about how we are addressing their concerns builds trust. Continuously iterating and updating the product based on feedback ensures we improve user satisfaction."

60. How do you manage the integration of new technologies into your product?

Answer: "Integrating new technologies involves thorough research, planning, and collaboration. I start by evaluating the potential benefits and feasibility of the technology. Collaborating with the engineering team helps assess integration requirements and challenges. Creating a detailed plan that outlines steps, timelines, and responsibilities ensures smooth implementation. Regular testing and monitoring ensure the new technology enhances the product without disrupting existing functionalities."

Sample Questions and Answers for Product Designers

61. How do you handle design critique?

Answer: "I welcome design critiques as they provide valuable perspectives and help improve the quality of my work. During critiques, I listen carefully, take notes, and ask clarifying questions to fully understand the feedback. I then analyse the suggestions and decide which changes align with the project goals and user needs. Iterating based on constructive feedback ensures the final design is well-rounded and effective."

62. What steps do you take to understand user needs and behaviours?

Answer: "Understanding user needs and behaviours begins with user research. I conduct interviews, surveys, and usability tests to gather qualitative insights. I also analyse quantitative data from analytics tools to observe user behaviour patterns. Creating user personas and journey maps helps me empathize with users and design solutions that meet their needs effectively."

63. Describe a project where you had to balance user needs with business goals.

Answer: "In a recent project, the business goal was to increase subscription rates for a SaaS product. However, user feedback indicated that the onboarding process was confusing. I redesigned the onboarding experience to be more intuitive and user-friendly, which addressed the user pain points. This balance led to a smoother user experience, and we saw a significant increase in trial-to-subscription conversions, aligning with the business goal."

64. How do you approach designing for accessibility?

Answer: "Designing for accessibility involves following best practices like using sufficient colour contrast, providing text alternatives for non-text content, and ensuring keyboard navigability. I also conduct accessibility audits using tools like Axe and include users with disabilities in usability testing. My goal is to create inclusive designs that are usable by everyone, regardless of their abilities."

65. What is your process for incorporating feedback from cross-functional teams?

Answer: "I incorporate feedback from cross-functional teams by organizing regular check-ins and design reviews. During these sessions, I present my designs and invite feedback from developers, product managers, and other stakeholders. I prioritize feedback based on its alignment with user needs and project goals. Collaborative tools like Figma and Miro help streamline this process, allowing everyone to contribute and stay informed."

66. How do you ensure your design decisions align with business objectives?

Answer: "Aligning design decisions with business objectives starts with a deep understanding of the company's goals and target metrics. I work closely with product managers and stakeholders to define success criteria for each project. Throughout the design process, I continually reference these objectives, ensuring my solutions address both user needs and business goals. Using metrics like conversion rates, user engagement, and retention helps evaluate and iterate on designs to achieve desired outcomes."

67. Describe a time when you had to advocate for a user-cantered design approach.

Answer: "In a project where the business team prioritized quick feature rollouts, I noticed that user experience was being compromised. I conducted user research and usability tests to gather evidence of the issues users were facing. I then presented these findings to the team, highlighting how improving UX could lead to higher user satisfaction and retention. By showing the long-term benefits and using concrete data, I successfully advocated for a more user-cantered approach, which ultimately improved our product's success."

68. What is your approach to designing for different platforms (e.g., web, mobile)?

Answer: "Designing for different platforms requires understanding the unique characteristics and constraints of each. I start by identifying the primary use cases and user behaviours for each platform. For web, I focus on responsive design principles to ensure the experience is consistent across devices. For mobile, I prioritize simplicity and touch-friendly interactions. I use platform-specific guidelines (e.g., Material Design for Android, Human Interface Guidelines for iOS) to ensure my designs feel native. Prototyping and user testing on actual devices help validate and refine the designs."

69. How do you integrate feedback from user testing into your designs?

Answer: "User testing is integral to my design process. After conducting tests, I analyse the feedback to identify patterns and key insights. I prioritize issues based on their impact on user experience and feasibility of changes. I then iterate on the design, making necessary adjustments and improvements. It's important to test the updated designs again to ensure the changes effectively address the feedback. This iterative process helps create a more user-friendly and effective product."

70. Can you explain a complex design concept to someone without a design background?

Answer: "Sure. Let's take the concept of 'responsive design.' Essentially, responsive design ensures that a website looks and works well on all devices, from desktops to smartphones. Think of it like water in a container. The water (content) adapts to the shape of the container (screen size). This means adjusting layouts, images, and text sizes so that users have a good experience no matter what device they use. This way, we make sure the website is accessible and functional for everyone."

71. How do you approach user research for a new design project?

Answer: "For a new design project, I start by understanding the project goals and target audience. I use a mix of qualitative and quantitative methods, such as interviews, surveys, and user observations. Creating user personas and journey maps helps visualize user needs and pain points. Analysing this data provides insights that inform design decisions and ensure the product meets user expectations."

72. Describe a time when you had to design for accessibility.

Answer: "In a previous project, we needed to ensure our web application was accessible to users with disabilities. I followed WCAG guidelines and conducted accessibility audits. Implementing features like keyboard navigation, screen reader compatibility, and high-contrast modes ensured inclusivity. Testing with users who have disabilities provided valuable feedback, leading to a more accessible and user-friendly design."

73. How do you balance creativity with functionality in your designs?

Answer: "Balancing creativity with functionality involves aligning design aesthetics with user needs and usability principles. I start by defining the core functionalities and user goals. Exploring creative concepts that enhance user experience while maintaining usability ensures a balanced design. Iterative testing and gathering feedback help refine the design, ensuring it is both visually appealing and functional."

74. What methods do you use to stay updated with design trends?

Answer: "Staying updated with design trends involves continuous learning and engagement with the design community. I follow design blogs, attend webinars, and participate in conferences. Engaging with platforms like Dribble and Behance provides inspiration and insights into emerging trends. Regularly experimenting with new tools and techniques helps me stay current and innovative in my designs."

75. Describe your experience with creating a design system.

Answer: "Creating a design system involves establishing a cohesive set of design standards and components. In one project, I led the development of a design system to ensure consistency across our product suite. Defining typography, colour palettes, and UI components provided a unified look and feel. Documenting guidelines and collaborating with cross-functional teams ensured the design system was effectively implemented and maintained."

76. How do you handle feedback on your designs?

Answer: "Handling feedback involves listening, empathizing, and being open to constructive criticism. I actively seek feedback from users, stakeholders, and team members. Analysing feedback to identify patterns and areas for improvement helps refine the design. Iterating based on feedback ensures the final design meets user needs and stakeholder expectations. Maintaining a collaborative and open-minded approach helps create better outcomes."

77. What is your approach to designing for different platforms (web, mobile, etc.)?

Answer: "Designing for different platforms involves understanding the unique characteristics and constraints of each. I start by defining the user experience and goals for each platform. Creating responsive designs and using flexible grids ensures consistency across devices. Testing on various platforms and gathering user feedback helps optimize the design for different contexts. This approach ensures a seamless and cohesive experience for users."

78. How do you ensure your designs align with brand guidelines?

Answer: "Ensuring alignment with brand guidelines involves understanding the brand's identity, values, and visual standards. I start by reviewing the brand guidelines and incorporating key elements like typography, colour schemes, and imagery into my designs. Regularly communicating with the brand team and seeking their feedback ensures consistency. This approach ensures the designs reflect the brand's identity and resonate with the target audience."

79. Describe a time when you had to design under tight deadlines.

Answer: "In a previous role, we had a tight deadline to launch a new feature. I started by prioritizing key design elements and creating a clear action plan. Collaborating closely with the team and maintaining open communication helped us stay on track. Despite the tight timeline, we delivered a high-quality design by focusing on essentials and iterating quickly based on feedback."

80. What is your approach to prototyping and testing designs?

Answer: "Prototyping and testing involve creating interactive mock-ups and gathering user feedback. I use tools like Sketch, Figma, and Invision to create prototypes. Conducting usability tests with target users helps identify pain points and areas for improvement. Iterating based on test results ensures the final design is user-friendly and effective. This approach validates design decisions and enhances user experience."

81. How do you incorporate user feedback into your designs?

Answer: "Incorporating user feedback involves gathering insights through surveys, interviews, and usability tests. I prioritize feedback based on its impact on user experience and alignment with project goals. Creating user stories and incorporating them into the design process ensures feedback is actionable. Regularly iterating and testing the design based on feedback helps refine and improve the final product."

82. Describe your experience with collaborative design tools.

Answer: "I have extensive experience with collaborative design tools like Figma, Miro, and Adobe XD. These tools facilitate real-time collaboration and feedback, making it easier to work with cross-functional teams. Using these tools, I can share designs, gather input, and iterate quickly. Collaborative design tools enhance communication and streamline the design process, leading to more efficient and effective outcomes."

83. How do you handle design constraints (e.g., technical limitations, budget)?

Answer: "Handling design constraints involves understanding and working within the given limitations. I start by identifying the constraints and assessing their impact on the design. Collaborating with the engineering and product teams helps find creative solutions that balance design goals with technical feasibility. Prioritizing key features and focusing on the most impactful elements ensures we deliver a high-quality design within constraints."

84. What is your approach to designing for internationalization and localization?

Answer: "Designing for internationalization and localization involves creating flexible and adaptable designs that cater to different languages and cultures. I start by understanding the target markets and their unique needs. Designing with scalable layouts and allowing for text expansion ensures compatibility. Collaborating with local experts and conducting usability tests with target users helps create a user-friendly experience. This approach ensures the product is accessible and relevant to diverse audiences."

85. How do you measure the success of your designs?

Answer: "Measuring the success of designs involves tracking key metrics and gathering user feedback. I use analytics tools to monitor user engagement, conversion rates, and satisfaction scores. Conducting usability tests and surveys provides qualitative insights. Regularly reviewing these metrics and iterating based on findings ensures the design meets user needs and business goals. This data-driven approach helps continuously improve the design."

www.ingramcontent.com/pod-product-compliance
Lightning Source LLC
LaVergne TN
LVHW051658050326
832903LV00032B/3885